Contractors-How To Get More Jobs In A Tough Economy

By John G Brewer

Legal Disclaimer

For legal purposes I cannot guarantee you will make any money using the methods laid out within.

The method laid out here is off of my own testing and results.

You may have different results than I do.

I am showing you what I have done and what is currently working for me.

The content within is solely my property.

Use it personally to your heart's content.

Just please do not use or share or abuse the content within.

Copyright © 2000 - 2012
©2012 John Brewer. All rights reserved. This book contains materials that have been created, developed, or commissioned by, and published with the permission of, John Brewer. (the "Materials") and this site and any such Materials are protected by international copyright and trademark laws.

Contractors-How To Get More Jobs In A Tough Economy

Index:

Legal Disclaimer

Contractors-How To Get More Jobs In A Tough Economy

Contractors-How To Get Even More Jobs In A Tough Economy

Hourly Rate

Quoted Jobs

Having Your Quotation Accepted

Payments

Contractors -How To Build A Huge Customer Base From Scratch

Real Estate Companies

Employing Help

Writing A Successful Flyer

My Successful Flyer

Advertising Yourself

Client Reviews and Testimonials

About the author

In Summary

Contractors-How To Get More Jobs In A Tough Economy

(How to get people to use your services even in tough times)

If you follow these guidelines you will get a lot more jobs and customers than you ever thought possible.

- *Focus on customer wants-*

(a) Ask them how you can help them.

Just remember all the time that you are there for their needs not your own.

When I was starting out many years ago as a young builder I missed this point and I used to tell customers what I thought that they wanted, this will cause some people to use a different tradesman to you..

It is ok if they ask you for suggestions. You can then give them some suggestions and ask them what they think.

(b) What is it that they actually want? (listen very carefully).

Remember it's what they want (very important).

(c) Be very clear about their wants.

If you are not really sure what it is they want ask more questions.

(d) Be honest with them, if you cannot help them, be up front and tell them so.

It may not be something that you are comfortable doing (different trade).

    (e) Suggest where they could go for further help to solve their problem.

(Different Tradesman or if you don't know tell them they will appreciate your honesty.)

    (f) Only suggest another Contractor if you know their work and service is good or it may come back to bite you.

- *When they leave you a message or text get back to them as soon as possible.*

    (a) Call them back and arrange to meet them as soon as possible.

It is very important to get back to your prospect ASP as they will call someone else very quickly if they don't know you and you do not get back to them quickly.

    (b) If you can't reach them leave a message stating what time you will call them back.

    (c) Always follow up your call at the time that you promised (this is very important).

- *Arrange a meeting time to suit <u>them</u>, it makes them feel important.*

(a) Try and fit your other jobs around it.

If they are getting prices from your competition the weighing factor could be the tradesman that fits in with them.

(b) Usually the earlier you can meet them the better chance you will have of getting them as a client.

In my earlier days I lost a few clients because I did not get back to them quick enough.

(c) Turn up at least 1 minute early.

A lot of people won't wait for you, be early.

- *Always introduce yourself on your first meeting (a handshake).*

(a) Don't talk about yourself unless they ask you a question about you.

(b) Give them facts about what you do truthfully as people can sense if you exaggerate.

(c) Let them know of successful work you have done especially around their areas.

(d) Never tell them about work that went wrong.

(e) Always be very positive even if they are negative.

(f) Give them the centre of attention

(g) Comment on their nice property if suitable.

(h) Refer to **Focus on customer wants**

- *Offer them a quotation if possible an (estimate can cause problems later on).*

(a) Send them a quotation as soon as possible either snail mail or email

(phone quotes are not as good).

(b) Follow up 2 days later if you have not heard from them.

Ask them questions-

- What they thought of your quote ?
- Did they get other quotes?
- Was your quote much higher than the one they accepted; if not was there a reason that they accepted the other quote?

Depending on their answers you may need to adjust the way you quote your work once you know why you missed out. If you don't ask you may never know.

This may be uncomfortable for you to begin with but will make you tens of thousands of dollars in the future.

I used to make a game out of it to make it more comfortable.

I would make up a list of questions and see how I could improve my results each time.

This method alone has created a 95% success rate of getting more customers and jobs.

I now find if they do not accept my quote that they usually don't go ahead with the work with anyone else anyway (they can't afford it).

> (c) Working on an hourly rate can cause problems.

Working on an hourly rate can lose you work.

Let's say you told them $50.00 per hour and someone else comes in at $45.00 per hour. You would probably lose the contract.

But let's assume you offer to quote them so as they know exactly what it will cost them.

In the section on **Quoted jobs** I explain how your hourly rate will be a lot higher in a quote.

> (d) An hourly rate works after they get to know your work.

Once they see how you work they usually don't mind paying your hourly rate.

> (e) A quotation lets them know exactly what the job will cost them and they will be more likely to employ your services.

- *When they accept your quote give them a start date*

and stick to it.

    (a) If something goes wrong and you can't get there on time give them as much notice as possible and re schedule the job (this tip alone is very powerful).

    (b) Ask for an upfront payment to lock them in (10%).

An upfront payment is for buying some of the materials required for the job, so it is accepted practice to ask before you start.

- *Build rapport with your customer*

    (a) This is covered in **Focus on customer wants** and **Always introduce yourself on your first meeting (a handshake)**

    (b) Making them feel important can build a long lasting relationship.

    (c) Always ask them if you can do anything else for them.

- *Ask for referrals*

    (a) Always ask your client if they know of anyone else that may require your services (this is another very powerful way of getting more customers).

(b) Hand them a couple of your business cards for them to hand out.

- *Are they happy with the work you have done for them?*

    (a) When you have completed the job ask your customer if they are pleased with the workmanship.

    (b) If not you must correct it to make them happy (you will occasionally get a picky one).

    (c) Ask them what they like about the job best.

    (d) How could you have achieved a better result?

- *Ask for payment*

    (a) How would they like to pay for the job?

    (b) You must always ask for payment when you are finished the job.

    (95% of the time if you ask you will get paid on the spot.)

    (c) If you have followed all the steps so far you will be able to bring a final invoice to the job with you (this is well worth the effort).

Contractors-How To Get Even More Jobs In A Tough Economy

(How to get even more people to use your services even in tough times)

- For a start don't be choosey (be prepared to do anything to build a client base).

When I first started as a builder in NZ and again in Australia I advertised as a home handyman which included mowing lawns and weeding gardens.

Yes I know tradesmen don't want to do lawns and gardens.

- My first 23 jobs in Australia were gardening of some sort or unrelated jobs.

Out of these I started building a solid client base and as they got to know me I received a lot of building work returning me many thousands of dollars.

Now these people could find builders but could not find anyone to weed their garden or hang a picture for them. Because I went that extra mile for them they employed me to do all their work plus told their friends and family about me which expanded my customer base when other trades people found the market place too competitive.

- I have made as much as $100 cash in an hour gardening (quoted).

- Many many times I have earned $50 plus in an hour

and in cash doing garden work plus many referrals.

- The main point here is you **need** a client list to be successful.

- Always go look at a job no matter how small it may be.

- Always do these small jobs for people especially for the elderly as they will really appreciate your time and effort and will reward you in the long run.

- These small jobs usually lead to larger work and referrals.

I have done a lot of small jobs which have cost me money but in the long run I have gained many many more clients and made a lot of money by doing these.

In 2011 I had a look at a very small tiling job (it took me 20 minutes to do).

The lady had rung nine tradesmen and only 2 of these turned up.

One of these told her the job was too small for him and the other promised to send her a quote (which he never did).

I did the job on the spot which led to thousands of dollars of future work and several referrals in her street.

These tips applied to me as a builder, maintenance man (handy man) but I see no reason you could not apply these to most contracting businesses.

The main points are really treating your customer well as you would like to be treated yourself.

By keeping your client in mind all the time there is absolutely no reason why you cannot become super successful.

Building rapport with them is vital for continued success as you become the trusted person that they call when they have a problem.

- If you only think of the money you can make out of them you will come unstuck.

You may get the first job but no more and no referrals which is the lifeblood of a successful client list.

Calling them up occasionally reminds them that you are still in business and can lead to more work.

I know that people used to say to me "give me a call when you are not busy and I may have some more work for you."

In later years I started keeping a client book with one section headed up 'people to call when I need more work'.

In the same book I indexed it A to Z with client details;

Client………………………

Phone …………………………..

Mobile…………………………..

Address………………………….

Comments ……………………..

Over the years I have often picked up extra when work coming in has been slow by contacting people from my client book.

Hourly Rate

If you must use an hourly rate keep it low to attract the customer.

As an example if the going rate is say $50.00 per hour charge $40.00 but let them know that you would rather quote the job if possible.

Also let them know that you have kept your rate low so as they can experience your workmanship and get you back to do more jobs for them at a later date.

This will get you extra clients on your list.

If you have followed all the above information you will get more quoted jobs after this which will enable you to gain a higher rate in your quote of say $55.00-$60.00(see quoted jobs)

I have found that giving estimates for jobs can have its problems but there are times when you will have to give an estimate. Where possible follow this up with a firm quote.

Over the years I have experimented with hourly rates and quoting and have found that my methods create thousands of dollars more per year.

Quoted jobs

When you quote your jobs you will allow a higher hourly rate which will more than make up for the straight hourly rate that you have charged previously.

Caution, don't be too greedy or you will lose the job and probably the prospect as well.

For example if the going rate is say $50.00 per hour I would allow $55-$60(I will show you how to increase this later).

You would then price your job using standard retail prices.

Quoting jobs properly takes some practice so if you haven't done this before take your time and get it right. It is beyond the scope of this book to show you how to do it right but there are many guides out there to help you.

If you have priced the job correctly you would be making an hourly rate of say $60.00 per hour plus 10% on material cost. Just remember this is for pricing jobs in tough times so don't be greedy. If you get the quote to the prospect within 2 days you should have a 80% chance of scoring the job.

Having Your Quotation Accepted

Ok you have had your quote accepted.

The first thing to do now is to quickly go over your quote to make shore everything is covered. If you find that you have under priced it you need to tell your client immediately.

Set a start date with your client and stick to it.

Always ask them if it would suit them for you to start--------.

Thank them.

Now this is the fun part (after your quote has been accepted).

Get out the list of materials and start looking around for cheaper prices.

You can do this by contacting the suppliers and asking for a better rate than their opposition (I have made extra money on just about every quoted job by using this method making hundreds or even thousands of dollars extra).

You can see now why I love quoting work.

Your clients are very happy because you were very professional and are getting the job.

Done and they know exactly how much it will cost them.

Payments

Ask for reasonable progress payments (you can ask for an upfront payment for materials if you wish).

If you have sub contractors working for you will be able to keep them happy with progress payments.

Always ask your clients are they happy with your work before you ask for any payment.

At the completion of any contract once again ask if they are happy with the job then say 'how would you like to pay for this?'

If you do not ask for payment they will put you on their list of pay later bills which could be next Month or more as they get the impression you are not in a hurry for your money.

Ask for referrals, leave your card and always thank them.

Contractors -How To Build A Huge Customer Base From Scratch

(How to build a huge customer base even in tough times)

The following methods are how I built a solid customer base starting day one in a new Country without knowing anyone.

On the very first day I could not sleep so I got out of bed at 4am and printed off about 200 flyers (see flyer below).

I started walking around the neighbourhood about 5.30 am dropping flyers in letterboxes.

Walking around got me familiar with the area right off.

Before I got back home my mobile rang with my first prospect.

Imagine their surprise when I arrived at their doorstep at 7.30 am.

By using my method described in (**Contractors-How To Get More Jobs In A Tough Economy**) I scored my first customer and job.

After finishing their small job that day I got home and immediately printed off about another 500 flyers which I dropped the following day. This resulted in another 3 calls and 3 new customers.

I continued this method over the weeks ahead and delivered approximately 5,000 flyers building up a great knowledge of the area and customer base. I now purchase my flyers to save myself time.

Real Estate Companies

Another type of client that I would target is Real Estate offices.

I found it difficult to get in with good companies but to get in with only one will pay off huge dividends if they handle rental properties.

I have got ongoing work from one company that looks after over one hundred properties.

The maintenance on these properties is ongoing as tenants move in and out.

The important point to remember here is that you must gain their trust.

You must be very reliable.

You must do a good job.

These property managers are very busy people and they don't want to hear your problems.

They just want someone that they can trust to carry out the maintenance on these properties with little fuss and worry.

If you can fit this roll you will be very successful indeed.

Companies will usually not pay you at the finish of the job but rather the 20th of the Month or the end of the Month but it is ongoing income.

Even in the toughest of times these rentals need upkeep.

Employing Help

Employing labour can cause all sorts of problems in today's world.

There are several ways you can go about this to avoid stress.

- Labour only is where you employ someone by the hour as a sub contractor.

This can be a great method as you are not responsible for their holiday pay etc. You just employ them by the hour or just for the job.

- Joint venture.

This is where you swap hours with another tradesperson like yourself.

Say you do 10 hours for him and he does 10 hours for you.

This way no money changes hands which are obviously a great advantage.

You just need to be a bit careful here that you both work similar otherwise it can cause a bit of friction.

- Insurance.

In all cases you need to be insured against anyone being injured on your job as well as damages to property. You can cover all of this with a standard 'Contractors Public Liability Insurance'.

Writing A Successful Flyer

Now there is no guarantee that all the information that I use on my flyers will work for all of you but by using most of these ideas you will increase your chances incredibly.

I have listed the main points in order of preference.

- Your business name (should have some reference as to what you do).

- 'Service With A Smile ' (many comments from clients on this, convinced them to call me)

- What service you are supplying.

- Home phone and mobile (a lot of elderly people will not call a mobile phone).

- Promises, see below (make sure you keep them).

- Let them know that you will call them back.

- Free quotations (people love free stuff).

- Customer satisfaction (let them know if they are not happy they do not pay).

- Always thank them for their business.

- Your experience (be truthful, people can tell if you are not telling the truth).

- Where you are from (your country, this will work if the area you are working have a lot of your fellow country people (If you don't know leave this out).

My Successful Flyer

John The Maintenance Man
Service with a Smile.

Phone; Home - xxxxxx   **Mobile - xxxxxx**

Hi, I am a semi retired Builder from New Zealand living in your area. I am doing Household repairs, small Building jobs, Lawn and Garden maintenance at a reasonable rate in your area.

<u>*My promise to you*</u> - I offer immediate quick quality service.
- I will return your call ASP.
- Free quotations-- I will guarantee my work
- I will go all out to meet you on time
- (if you are not happy you do not pay)

Thank you for your business.
ABN   xxxxxxxxx   Email- xxxxxxxxxxxxxxxxxxxxxx

Advertising Yourself

As well as doing flyer drops a website should be considered in today's market place.

In the next section I have listed two simple websites that have created me more customers.

These are free sites where people looking for your types of services in your area can also find you.

You will see where happy customers have left their reviews and testimonials regarding my services.

These are genuine reviews by genuine happy people.

Do not ever try and fake this as it will not work.

Client Reviews and Testimonials

http://www.tradecritic.com.au/region/29/52/1

Job Description: Renovation and repairs
"A true professional who takes pride in his work"
Date Of Service: 2011-05-10
★ ★ ★ ★ ★
Reviewed By: ROSIE
Review: John completed some renovations and interiors repairs for me. He took the time to listen to my ideas and came up with great solutions. The quality of work is 5 star. His attitude was professional, friendly, punctual. I would recommend John to anyone who needs a builder for home renovations.
Posted on: 2011-07-18
Did you find this review helpful? Yes
0 people found this review helpful
Report Offensive Content

Job Description: Maintenance job
"Excellent"
Date Of Service: 2011-06-07
★ ★ ★ ★ ★
Reviewed By: Petal
Review: John did an excellent job for me not only maintaining my garden for me but also doing some small fix up jobs around the house. I was really impressed that he willingly went about doing these little jobs that most other tradesmen avoid. His price was really reasonable, he was punctual and he did a really good job. My lawns and hedges look really great, and I am happy now that all those niggly jobs at home are done.
Posted on: 2011-06-23
Did you find this review helpful? Yes
1 people found this review helpful
Report Offensive Content

Job Description: excellent
"excellent"
Date Of Service: 2011-06-09
★ ★ ★ ★ ★
Reviewed By: sheena29
Review: John looks after our lawns at our flat. He always arrives on time, is quick and does a great job every time. I would recommend him to everyone
Posted on: 2011-06-20
Did you find this review helpful? Yes
1 people found this review helpful
Report Offensive Content

Job Description: plastering and house repairs
"Great service"
Date Of Service: 2011-06-10

★ ★ ★ ★ ★

Reviewed By: JoJo
Review: At last a tradie who came on time, was patient and fixed my problems. He went the extra mile to get the tools needed to complete my job. Thank you John
Posted on: 2011-06-15
Did you find this review helpful? Yes
1 people found this review helpful
Report Offensive Content

http://www.tradecritic.com.au/region/29/46/1

Latest Reviews (7 in total)

Job Description: Building, Tiling, Door Fitting, Insulation, Gyprock
"Reliable, Punctual, Meticulous, Trustworthy"
Date Of Service: 2011-10-03

★ ★ ★ ★ ★

Reviewed By: shazzamataz01
Review: I am extremely happy with John's work. He did every thing I asked for and more. He finished the job completely without anything left undone. I have been trying to get this job done for 2.5 years and that was just finding a Builder that would show up and give me a quote. I would have no hesitation in recommending John for any job around the home. He is marvellous.
Posted on: 2011-10-05
Did you find this review helpful? Yes
1 people found this review helpful
Report Offensive Content

Job Description: REBUILT & PAINTED PART OF BALCONY
"TRUSTWORTHY PROFESSIONAL"
Date Of Service: 2011-07-27

★ ★ ★ ★ ★

Reviewed By: sandra
Review: John is a nice easy going person to deal with and very professional with excellent workmanship. You can see he takes pride in his work and I would not hesitate to use him again or reccommend him. A gentleman.
Posted on: 2011-08-03
Did you find this review helpful? Yes
1 people found this review helpful
Report Offensive Content

Job Description: internal walls
"impressive"
Date Of Service: 2011-07-22

★ ★ ★ ★ ★

Reviewed By: MacDonald
Review: John arrived on time. His workmanship is excellent! We are very impressed with his attention to detail and fast service. We are very happy with his work and would not hesitate to have his building services again. A+++
Posted on: 2011-07-22

Did you find this review helpful? Yes
1 people found this review helpful
Report Offensive Content

Job Description: Curtain rods/picture hanging
"Completely satisfied with work done"
Date Of Service: 2011-06-23

★ ★ ★ ★ ★

Reviewed By: GillianB
Review: John was happy to consider a small job and work in with myself and my landlord. We are now getting John back for some other work we need done. He's now our 'go to' handyman when we need one.
Posted on: 2011-07-11
Did you find this review helpful? Yes
1 people found this review helpful
Report Offensive Content

Job Description: Tiling, Concreting, Guttering
"Very impressed"
Date Of Service: 2011-05-04

★ ★ ★ ★ ★

Reviewed By: Lindsay
Review: A really top quality job for a reasonable price... John was punctual and communicated all aspects of what needed to be done, and when he had to spend a little extra time, was happy to remain firm on his quoted price... Exceptional work... :-)
Posted on: 2011-06-22
Did you find this review helpful? Yes
1 people found this review helpful
Report Offensive Content

Job Description: Install timber/glass doors.
"Gets the Job Done On Time"
Date Of Service: 2011-06-14

★ ★ ★ ★ ★

Reviewed By: KessaG
Review: For me the most outstanding attributes of John's work ethic were: He did not treat me like the village idiot just because I am a woman. He was always punctual and polite. Remarkable! He just got on with the job, not answering his mobile every 10 minutes. Also remarkable. He took pride in his work and charged a reasonable rate. I would recommend John for any of your handyman needs. Coombabah Resident
Posted on: 2011-06-17
Did you find this review helpful? Yes
1 people found this review helpful
Report Offensive Content

Job Description: excellent
"Fantastic, couldnt be happier"
Date Of Service: 2011-06-03

★ ★ ★ ★ ★

Reviewed By: sheena
Review: I would recommend the maintenance man to everyone!! He was on time, quick and efficient and the job was done to a top quality standard. He was friendly and very well priced. Its nice to have a trades person to call on that I can trust
Posted on: 2011-06-15
Did you find this review helpful? Yes
1 people found this review helpful
Report Offensive Content

About the author

John Brewer was a successful self employed Builder in NZ for 37 years and by using these methods kept up a good client base.

Even in times of economic hardship when other Builders ran out of work he had a continuous flow of work.

When other trades people had to travel out of town to find work he never had to.

He retired at the age of 57 a wealthy man with financial and time freedom.

Unfortunately the huge share market crash and property market crash did a lot of damage to his portfolio and he again entered the building trade in 2010.

In 2010 he travelled to Australia's Gold Coast to start a home maintenance business.

At that time the Gold Coast was in a recession caused by the decline in tourism and a lot of Tradesmen were travelling out of town looking for work.

By employing the following methods he started a new customer base the very first day of business with 1 job the first day and 3 on the second.

He now once again has a solid customer base on the Gold Coast where he now lives with his wife Jean.

In Summary

If you follow the guide lines given in this book you will certainly build a solid customer base. You will also enjoy continuing work coming in even in the toughest of times.

You need to keep building your customer base as you will find some of your customers dropping off your list for many reasons.

Some of these may be –moving away, death, family member or friend starting in opposition to you etc.

Good luck,

Regards, John Brewer

Copyright © 2000 - 2012
©2012 John Brewer. All rights reserved. This book contains materials that have been created, developed, or commissioned by, and published with the permission of, John Brewer. (the "Materials") and this site and any such Materials are protected by international copyright and trademark laws

www.ingramcontent.com/pod-product-compliance
Lightning Source LLC
Chambersburg PA
CBHW061522180526
45171CB00001B/296